REFERRAL HARVESTER

A Proven Strategy for Compounding Your Client Base

Tiana Wilson-Buys

authorHOUSE®

AuthorHouse™ UK
1663 Liberty Drive
Bloomington, IN 47403 USA
www.authorhouse.co.uk
Phone: 0800.197.4150

© 2016 Tiana Wilson-Buys. All rights reserved.

No part of this book may be reproduced, stored in a retrieval system, or transmitted by any means without the written permission of the author

Published by AuthorHouse 03/23/2016

ISBN: 978-1-5246-2998-4 (sc)
ISBN: 978-1-5246-2997-7 (e)

Print information available on the last page.

Any people depicted in stock imagery provided by Thinkstock are models, and such images are being used for illustrative purposes only. Certain stock imagery © Thinkstock.

This book is printed on acid-free paper.

Because of the dynamic nature of the Internet, any web addresses or links contained in this book may have changed since publication and may no longer be valid. The views expressed in this work are solely those of the author and do not necessarily reflect the views of the publisher, and the publisher hereby disclaims any responsibility for them.

DEDICATION

To Philippa Wilson-Buys for all your support
and for being living proof that one referral
can change the course of one's life

And to Glyn Bricknell for your guidance, encouragement
and nurturing me all those years ago

PRAISE FOR THE REFERRAL HARVESTER SYSTEM

"I love it. It's so versatile that someone, like myself, can adapt it if they are not particularly systems orientated. The concept lends itself to all styles of working. Whilst I've not adopted all of the system yet, I have adopted the categorising of prospects to advocates and adapted my approach to establishing relationships, follow up and deepening advocate relationships, in order to improve referrals. I'm also much more up front and focused about what I want out of business relationships.

The biggest thing I've gained from implementing the Referral Harvester is focus. I now have purpose and objectives for business relationships and networking. My feedback helps me to understand who will help me to sell my business objectives and I still have the enjoyment of building relationships."

Beverly S. - Organisation Development Consultant based in the UK.

"Easy to use system which is now an integral part of my business. In fact, I can't think how I would run my business without my Referral Harvester"

Andrew B - Real Estate Broker on the south coast of South Africa

"As soon as I learnt about the Referral Harvester system I knew it was for me. I've always referred and connected people naturally, but in a random way and without asking for referrals in return.

The Referral Harvester not only benefits me but also makes sure that I continue to support my clients' businesses in a meaningful and consistent way. By giving me a clear, structured approach to segmenting clients (ABCD), a step by step approach to educating them about the value (to me and them) of referrals and a regular series of 'touches' to make each month, I can manage the system easily.

Since going through the Referral Harvester I have seen a shift in the number and <u>quality</u> of referrals I receive as clients and associates now know exactly what I do and who I want to work with, so refer only those people who will be most interested in my services."

Joanne D. - Marketing Consultant and Content Marketing Specialist, based in the UK.

"Flippin' fantastic. It is so easy to understand and easy to implement. The effects are astronomic compared to the effort you put in to complete your Referral Harvester - I really enjoy doing it too! It feels good giving someone, for example, a link

to an article that I know they will enjoy or sending them a card."

Heather W. - Event Consultant and Manager, based in the UK.

"I learnt so many ways to ignite referrals from our long-term, current and new contacts. What a wealth of business in plain sight that I had up until now left un-nurtured and in the wilderness. Thank you Tiana, for a cost effective, time efficient boost to my business. I would recommend those new to business or long in the tooth to take a new look at referrals, it is amazing."

Wendy H. – Will Writer based in the North East of England.

"Clear and to the point. No wasted time or faffing about. A system that I can easily start using immediately"

Patricia B – International Lawyer based in the UK.

"I have never come across a systematic way to gather referrals from clients that I felt comfortable with and the Referral Harvester allows me to be professional and to follow a proven system whilst being true to myself and my values.

I felt relieved to find the Referral Harvester system as it came along at the right time and has helped me to move forward in my business when I felt stuck. I knew there had to be a better way to obtain referrals, a way that felt right and comfortable for me. A huge thank you!"

Kate M. - Healthcare Consultant based in the UK.

Tiana Wilson-Buys

"A logical, easy system. Why hadn't I thought of harvesting referrals in a systematic way before? The positive impact on my business has been phenomenal!"

Angela K, - Wholesaler in the Home Decor sector, based in the UK.

"A simple and effective (in both cost and time) way to recognise and develop potential business through referrals. Exactly what it says on the tin!!"

Emily M – Events Manager based in the North of England

CONTENTS

Introduction xiii

Chapter 1	What is The Money Value of a Referral? 1
Chapter 2	Building Your Database – as Easy as ABCD 7
Chapter 3	Capture and Qualify 17
Chapter 4	Educate Your Clients... 35
Chapter 5	Your Referral Harvester System is Based on The Personal Touch........................... 43
Chapter 6	Valuable Item: Leveraging the Sumimasen Philosophy......... 53
Chapter 7	Using Technology and Old-Time Charm in Harmony............................ 63
Chapter 8	The Magic of Face-to-Face Interaction.......... 69
Chapter 9	Putting It All Together 75
Chapter 10	Harvesting Time 81

About the Author.. 85

INTRODUCTION

I was 12 years old when I started my first business. I was breeding hamsters. Six female and one male hamster formed the core of this fledgling business. We lived in a small two-bedroom flat and my room was completely taken over by my business. Each hamster lived in its own cage and Stud (yes, really), the male got to move from female cage to female cage with short rest periods in between, in his own cage. He did need rest from time to time...

With six females producing an average of five babies in every litter, I had about 30 to sell every six weeks! I sold baby hamsters (pups) to all my friends at school and church and business was going very well. After a few months, I expanded my business to include cages, toys and feeding equipment. My mum took me to a pet wholesaler where I would buy cages, feeding tubes, dishes, wheels and anything else related to hamsters. Adding a small mark-up, I created "package deals". You could buy one hamster, cage, a bit of food, feeding tube, wheel and wood shavings for ZAR 5.00. (South African Rand) Bargain!

Then there were the wood shavings. If you know anything about hamsters, you'll know that they can be quite messy. In those days, we used wood shavings in the bottom of the cage to catch the mess and for the hamsters to nest in. The wood shavings had to be cleared out every few days and fresh wood shavings placed into the cage. Wood shavings for this purpose could be bought from the local pet shop at ZAR 0.20 per bag. I got the idea to approach a local joiner to find my own wood shavings. There was a large joinery company about a mile from our flat so I cycled up there one day and "negotiated" with the owner. Truth is, they were just binning the shavings in the skip every day, so didn't care if I wanted it. This meant I could cycle up there every few days and fill two bin bags with wood shavings. Tying them to my bike, I'd take them home and re-package into plastic shopping bags. Now I could supply my customers with wood shavings at ZAR 0.10 per bag! So, instead of one-off sales, I had a product my customers needed on an ongoing basis. Business was booming!

But, as you can imagine, there are only so many kids in my school and church. My business got to the point where everyone who wanted a hamster *had* a hamster. My market was drying up yet my females were still producing baby hamsters at lightning speed. Sure, I still sold wood shavings every week but very few hamsters. My business had struck a brick wall. (In hindsight, I should have just slowed down production but at 12 years of age, it just didn't occur to me).

And then I had a Eureka moment!

I spoke to all my regular customers and offered them a month's supply of wood shavings for each friend they introduced to me, who wanted to buy a hamster package. This opened up a whole new market to me. All these kids had friends in other schools, sports clubs, churches and family. They would happily bring new customers to me for a month's supply of wood shavings. They saved their pocket money (as they no longer had to pay for their continuous wood shaving needs) and I had new customers. Bear in mind the wood shavings didn't cost me anything either (just the time to collect from the joiner and the time it took to re-package into shopping bags).

As a new customer bought a hamster package from me, I would make the same offer to them. This resulted in constant referrals flowing into my business. My mum was roped in to help with deliveries since I now sold my products in a fairly wide geographical area. Every Saturday morning, we would load up the old, orange VW Beatle with hamster cages and set off to deliver them to my new customers. Some Saturdays we had to make more than one trip.

I made more money during those months than any other kid in my school. After feeding my hamsters, paying my mum for fuel (for deliveries), buying hamster vitamins and all other costs, I made an average profit of around ZAR15.00 per week! To put that into context, most kids received ZAR1.00 per week in pocket money, in those days. I still received my ZAR1.00 pocket money from Dad every week, and also had ZAR15.00 on top of that. I was rich! (or at least felt rich)

I did learn at least two things from this experience at the tender age of 12. Firstly, referrals can absolutely sky-rocket your business. I'm pretty sure the idea of referrals has been around for eons, but to me, at that point, I thought I had come up with an absolutely brilliant, bright, new idea. Secondly (in hindsight), I should have invested all the profit I made back then, instead of spending it on cool pencil cases, sweets and toys.

I am passionate about referrals and I have always focused on this part of business, throughout my life. In this book I want

Tiana Wilson-Buys

to share with you how you can leverage this phenomenon in your business.

To your referral success,

Tiana Wilson-Buys

2016

Chapter 1

What is The Money Value of a Referral?

This chapter was written to bring into focus the costs involved in finding new customers, as compared to the Referral Harvester system which is described in Chapters 2 - 10. If you want to dive into learning the system then move onto Chapter 2 now. You can always read this one after Chapter 10.

Let's not beat around the bush. For us as business owners, it is always all about the bottom line – we want to know what the return on our investment will be. Before committing to any new marketing, PR, sales training or new software for our business, we always investigate the potential returns. That is just plain business 101.

You want to get more sales for less money, as does every other business owner in the world. Many business owners calculate exactly what it costs them to gain one new sale and therefore one new client. They take into account things like sales team training, advertising, social media strategies and time invested to clinch the deal. All these things are extremely important and if you do take all of these factors into consideration, I congratulate you! You are part of the minority in the world of business owners. Many business owners have no idea as to what gaining a sale costs them. Let's do a simple exercise to calculate your cost per sale.

Action Time

Make a list of everything you have spent over the last 12 months on sales and marketing, including the amounts. Here are a few pointers to help you:

- Exhibition costs
- Print advertising costs
- Networking fees (membership and meeting fees)
- Social Media advertising
- PR (Public relations)
- Sales team training
- Leaflet printing and distribution
- Website hosting
- Direct mail marketing

Add together all the amounts you have spent on sales and marketing (more than you thought?). Now count up the number of sales you have made in that same time period. The last part of this simple calculation is to divide your total spend by the number of sales you generated.

Your calculation will look like this:

Marketing Spend / Number of Sales = Cost per sale

So, as an example, if you had spent £9790 on marketing and you generated 564 sales in that period of time, it cost you just over £17 to generate one sale. Look at your own calculation – is this what you expected?

But....it costs more than money

Over and above the monetary input to generate a sale, you also have a time and effort input. Typically, this will include the time to set up and exhibit at a business exhibition or time spent attending networking events. It will also include the time you spend on social media as well as organising a leaflet drop.

These are "energies" we spend and often forget to include in calculations. Your time and effort has a value. This you will be well aware of if you are employing a team member to take care of the sales and marketing. It all adds up in the end.

Let's look at your ROI from a different angle

Before you can calculate your ROI (Return on Investment) for any marketing strategy, you need to find the value of the "Return" part. In other words, what is a sale worth to you? Businesses differs greatly – service based, product based, flat rates or scaled rates. You might offer a service or product at a standard rate, so it's easy for you to know what an average sale is worth in monetary value.

If however, as in the case of most businesses, you offer various products or services at different prices, you will need to calculate the average value of a sale. Below is an easy exercise to help you with this calculation.

Action Time

Go back to your last hundred sales invoices (if you do not have one hundred, use however many you have). Add all the totals together and divide by 100 (or however many invoices you used). This will give you a rough idea of your average sale value. Profit margins are irrelevant at this point – we are working only with the gross value of your average sale.

Your calculation will look like this:

Total Gross Amount of 100 Sales / 100 = Average Value of Sale

Example: £11 892 / 100 = £118.92

Our example above shows that an average sale for this business is worth almost £119. What is an average sale worth to you?

Spending more than you need to?

Each industry has its own standards or parameters and a quick search online will give you a good idea of how much to spend on marketing, in your line of business. The general consensus is to have a marketing spend of between 2% and 10% of gross revenue. For slow and steady growth in your business, you might want to spend 2% to 5% on gaining new clients. If you are thinking of more rapid growth, you might need to re-invest 5% to 10% of your gross revenue.

Find a comfortable percentage for your business and then look back to the exercise you have just completed. You now know what an average sale is worth to you, so it is easy to work out the percentage of the amount you feel comfortable with. You should now have a much clearer view of how much to spend on attracting new clients.

Look back at what you are spending (as calculated at the beginning of this chapter) on marketing. Do these two figures correlate, or are you spending too much – or too little?

Spend less money, less time and get more sales

Isn't that exactly what you want? I have yet to meet one business owner who does not want to save time and money yet still attract more clients – and therefore more sales. If you can align with this sentiment, this book is for you.

Why do you allow your best salesperson to only bring you ONE sale?

What?! The question is outrageous, isn't it? The sad truth is that most business owners do exactly that – they allow their best salesperson to walk out the door after giving them only one sale.

Do you know who your best salesperson is? It is the client you served a minute ago. It is the guy walking out your shop door with a box of your widgets under his arm. It is the lady who just bought a service package from you. It is that happy client who has just experienced your great customer service, who had their problem solved by you or who had finally found that widget they had been looking for forever. Your *client* is your best salesperson.

At the exact time of transaction, you are providing your client with something they need or want. In that moment, your client is a very happy person indeed and they know it – they feel it. They also know, even at a subconscious level, that you are the cause of their happiness and satisfaction. Right in that moment, your best salesperson is born. All you need to do is leverage your client's happiness. It is easy to do, doesn't cost you much time or money but has the potential to sky-rocket your sales.

So, what's the catch?

You will be wondering why more business owners are not tapping into this method of attracting new clients. The answer is that most business owners do not even realise that their clients are their best salespeople. Those who do realise this fact may not know how to leverage their client's happiness and satisfaction.

During a recent survey of over 300 business owners in the UK, 61% admitted they NEVER ask for a referral from their clients. Of those that do ask, more than 38% NEVER follow up after asking for a referral. Less than 2% of business owners surveyed have an actual system through which they leverage their client's happiness and satisfaction.

The obvious solution is to implement a system whereby you can leverage your client's happiness and satisfaction, in order to gain new clients. The cherry on top of the cake is to do all of this without spending a great deal of time and money.

In the following chapters, you will learn how to build (Chapters 2 to 7) and implement (Chapters 8 to 11) your *Referral Harvester* machine. You will also hear from other business owners who share their lightbulb moments and experiences with the *Referral Harvester* system and how they implemented the *Referral Harvester* in their respective businesses.

Chapter 2

Building Your Database — as Easy as ABCD

We all have different filing systems – or non-existent filing systems. You might keep your client information in the form of their business cards, scattered around your office and desk drawers at random. Some business owners have an actual paper file for each of their clients. This might contain contact information and previous order information. Others still, might have a high-tech system where a full list of clients can be printed out with one mouse click.

What type of system you use in your business is not important. The important factor here is that you can lay your hands on all your client information. It is this information – which you already have at your disposal – which will be forming the basis of your new *Referral Harvester* machine.

Sorting your database – the ABCD's

It is now time to gather all your client information together, in one heap, so to speak. Make that printout or gather all those files together on a desk (or the floor, for that matter).

The next step is to sort the information into workable groups. I'm sure, as you look at the mess of information now staring you in the face, that you feel there is no way a system can be born from this. Let me put your mind at ease – creating a workable database from all this information is easy. In fact, it is as easy as ABCD.

All your clients can be divided into four groups, for the purpose of creating a workable database. These groups are:

- A - Your Advocates
- B – Below-peak education
- C – New Connection
- D – Delete

Who are your "A" clients – Advocates

Going through your list of clients, you will notice a few "gems". Usually we classify clients as "gems" when they place regular, large orders. This is indeed very important – it affects our bottom line, after all. We all want more clients who spend large amounts of money with us. Regular orders help us calculate our cash flow forecast. Knowing a client will probably place a large order every second month creates predictability. These are all very important factors in a client.

For the purpose of creating a workable database however, you need to view your clients through different lenses. There is another type of "gem". These "gems" are those clients who have referred other people to you. They might only use your services once in a while for themselves, but they have told their contacts about you – which leads to more business for you. I call these clients your Advocates. They are your fan club. They are happy with your service or product and feel the need to tell others about it. Your Advocates are the gems in your database.

Below Peak Education group

Your "B" group of clients are those clients who give you a great deal of business and you have a good relationship with them – they just haven't yet referred any of their contacts to you.

By reading this book, it is clear that you want more business and that you want to achieve this in a systematic manner – with a plan. You want to build your business, and you want to build it on referrals.

Your "B" group of clients are already familiar with your service or product, they have already experienced your great customer service and they support you on an ongoing basis. They just haven't yet been educated on how you run and build your business. They do not know what an important part referrals play in your business. They have some education with regards to you and your business – remember, they already know your product or service as well as how you treat your clients. But since they lack the knowledge of how you run and build your business (through referrals), they are yet to reach the peak of their education. That is why I call these clients the "Below Peak Education" group. They need a bit more education to fully appreciate how important referrals are to you and your business.

New Connections

All new clients land in the "C" group. They are new Connections. As you sign up a new client or handle a new order, you need to add this new client to your "C" list. They have just experienced their first interaction with your business – hopefully they are impressed and happy. They still have to experience your great customer care over the

Tiana Wilson-Buys

long term and they certainly have no education about how you run your business.

Setting up your new system for the first time, means you'll have to do some historical work here. In this group, you will add all those clients you have dealt with once or twice in the past, but who you are still to build a relationship with. These are typically clients who you know little about – in fact you are not even sure if they were truly happy with your service as your interactions with them have been quite limited.

You will need to find out more about your "C" group clients, qualify them (more about Qualifying in Chapter 3), build relationships with them and educate them.

"D" means Delete

Sorting your database also gives you the opportunity to do a bit of house cleaning. Going through all your client files, you might find a few clients belonging to the "D" group. These are clients you might as well Delete from your database. There might be a client who you know went out of business eight months ago – delete their file. The same goes for the client who you know moved their business away from your area and you are 99% sure you'll never do business with them again. Also in this group are those clients who ended their relationship with you on a bad note – unfortunately, there are always one or two in every business.

Your "Delete" group will consist of everyone you are pretty sure you'll never do business with again. Delete them and move on. There will be many other clients in your A, B and C groups to work with.

NOTE: You don't need to delete these customers from your regular client database. Delete in this sense means removal from your Referral Harvester database. In other words, you effectively have two databases, your regular client database and your Referral Harvester database.

Referral Harvester User Comment

Andrew B is a Real Estate Broker on the south coast in South Africa. He made a surprising discovery while sorting his client database into the ABCD groups.

"Years ago, I sold a small cottage to an older lady who was downsizing from her four-bedroom family home. She also owns and runs a small coffee shop on the edge of town. We have a good relationship and I often meet with clients and friends in her coffee shop."

"When I came upon her file, while sorting my database, I realised that she was an absolute gem! I was aware that she had referred new clients to me in the past, but never realised just how many. She chats to everyone coming into her coffee shop and is in a great position to refer newcomers to the town, to whoever they need. After further digging, I found that she had referred 19 new clients to me over the past eight years! Calculating the money value of her referrals was an eye-opener. I felt compelled to promptly buy her a huge bunch of flowers."

Action Time

Start sorting your clients into groups, as explained in this chapter. If you have a printed list of clients, you can just mark each client with the appropriate letter – A, B, C or D. If you have a heap of papers or files, sort them into different heaps – one for each group.

The easiest way to accomplish this task is to literally take it one step at a time. Look at each client in turn and ask yourself a few quick questions about the client. This will help you decide which group this client needs to be placed into. You can use the following questions as a check-list for each of your clients:

- Has this client ever referred a new client to me?
- Do I have a good relationship with this client?
- Can I realistically expect more business from this client?
- Do I believe this client had a good experience in dealing with my business?

If you come across a client who has already referred a new client to you, he or she obviously belongs amongst your Advocates. Should you also have a good relationship with this particular client, it will only add weight to their position in the "A" group. It can also be assumed that he or she had had a great experience in dealing with your business – or else they would not have referred one or more of their contacts to you.

There will be clients who have not yet referred anyone to you, but you do have a good relationship with them and you believe they have had a good experience when dealing with you. If you also believe future business with them is a possibility, these clients belong in the "B" group.

All new clients and those you do not yet have relationships with, fall into the "C" group. You do not know, at this point, whether they had a good experience in their dealings with your business. You also do not know if they will use your services again or if they will eventually refer a contact to you. The "C" group can be described as "The Great Unknown".

The "D" group is possibly the quickest and easiest to deal with. The biggest indicator that a client belongs to this group is if you know you'll probably never do business with them again. Are they still in business? Did our last interaction end on a negative note? Identify your "D" group clients and delete them from your database – certainly from a *Referral Harvester* perspective. You might want to keep their details for legal or tax purposes but they do not belong in your new *Referral Harvester* database.

In effect, you will have two databases; one for all your client information and one for only your *Referral Harvester* clients. So, a client might be "deleted" from your Referral Harvester database, but still remain on your main client database. (Detailed explanation in Chapter 3, Let's Qualify).

Referral Harvester User Comment

Beverly S. is an Organisation Development Consultant based in the UK. She found sorting her database was easy to do:

"I'm naturally a people person therefore I have people I've naturally connected with, whether that's because we've naturally gelled and have things in common; or because we are so different we are attracted by learning opportunities. These people I keep in my head as 'As' and' Bs' and contact them with articles, events or information they may be interested in.

I have lists as part of my mail service marketing – I keep them in my mailing software and in Excel. These are categorised by my business areas and then by whether they are A, B, C, or to be deleted. Some people are an A on one list and a B on another, simply by virtue of the work I do and their experience of it."

So, where are we now?

You now have three heaps of paper / files or possibly a printout with three groups of clients. You have one group of

Advocates or your fan club, another group needing further education and a final group of newbies – new clients who are yet to rise to the ranks of the "B" and "A" groups.

Your new *Referral Harvester* will work on the principal of moving each client up the ranks from "C" to "B" and finally to "A". There will be clients falling by the wayside, who will end up in the "D" group. These will be clients who progress to this group purely because they re-locate or find a new supplier – all the natural things which can lead to them becoming ex-clients. You will also find a few clients along the way, who might just not be interested in building a relationship with you. This happens – people differ – accept it and move on. You can still do business with them but they will just not form part of your *Referral Harvester*.

Referral Harvester User Comment

Mike M. is an Electrical Health and Safety Consultant based in the North of England.

"This was a revealing and almost a 'cleansing moment' sorting out the databases into A B C & D's; it not only put them into priority clients and contacts, but also highlighted which clients not to waste your time on – therefore focusing on the right clients. Obviously ALL my clients get excellent service, but now I know which ones to focus more on."

Referral Harvester User Comment

Kate M. is a Healthcare Consultant based in the UK.

"This was a real light bulb moment where I could see a workable system starting to emerge and how I could apply it to my business. I realised I needed to redo my database to get

it into the shape it needed to be, but I felt energised to do this as I could see the huge potential and pay off this would create."

With three heaps of files staring at you, you are now ready to start compiling and qualifying your database...

Chapter 3

Capture and Qualify

Picture a funnel. This is a "Y" shaped device used to control the flow of liquid into a container. The more liquid you pour into the top of the funnel, the more comes out the narrow end. The same principal is used in your *Referral Harvester*. You pour all your "A", "B" and "C" clients into your *Referral Harvester* Funnel, and referrals (and more sales) come out the narrow end of the funnel. During this chapter you will be creating your Funnel Spreadsheet and pouring all your client information into it.

Capture those ABC's

In the previous chapter, you did a lot of the hard work – gathering those files, printouts and business cards. Well done! You now have three groups of clients, namely:

- Advocates group
- Below-peak Education group
- New Connections

As we are all different and have various types of filing systems, it is now time to capture all the relevant client data into a workable format. The easiest format for our purposes is a basic Excel spreadsheet.

At this point in the process of creating your *Referral Harvester*, you need to be able to see your entire database at a glance. This will help you determine how many clients you have in your database, what their code (A, B or C) is, and make it easy to complete the next step – qualifying each client.

Referral Harvester User Comment

Pete G. and Andrew P. are international Marketing Consultants based in the UK.

"We use Google Drive for our Filter Funnel – it enables us to share with the team, and keep updated in Real Time. At a glance, we can see our clients' details and identify where new business is coming from."

Action Time

Create a basic Excel spreadsheet with the following columns:

- Client Name
- Code (A, B or C)
- Contact number / E-mail
- Last business contact date
- Last referral given
- Notes

Capture each client's information into your Funnel spreadsheet. Next to the client name, type in their code, which was allocated during the sorting of your database (see Chapter 2).

Your advocates will be coded with an "A", clients needing education are coded as "B" and new clients are in the "C" group. Type their contact number and e-mail address in the next column. This is needed as they will be contacted by phone or e-mail during the qualification process.

The fourth column is very important. Here you need to capture the date of their last business transaction with you. When was their last order placed with your business? This date is important because it will be referred to during the qualification process. You should be able to find this information on a copy of their invoice or in your financial software. If you don't keep this information, try to at least record the month of transaction from memory.

The next column is used for your Advocates. If you know this client has given you referrals in the past, try to remember who the last referral was. Type this information in the second to last column. The last column should be wider than the other columns in order to give you space to type notes during the qualifying process.

Image 1 is an example of a basic *Referral Harvester* Funnel

(Available for download from www.talkingbusiness.biz/RH)

Name	Code	Contact Details	Last Contact	Referral Given	Notes
Anton Jackson	B	XXX	4 Feb		
Raz Kohli	B	XXX	7 Feb		
Anne Rompford	A	XXX	20 Feb	Peter Andrews	
Peter Andrews	C	XXX	6 Mar		
Lynda Smith	C	XXX	7 Mar		

Your Funnel spreadsheet will be used continuously in the future. As you complete a transaction with a new client, their details should be captured into your funnel. Clients will also be moved from the funnel spreadsheet into your final *Referral Harvester* database, once they have been qualified.

Bear in mind that you will be building solid relationships with each of your Advocates – this is the aim of the Referral Harvester. It would be near impossible to build this type of relationship with hundreds of people. So be picky in who you allow to be on your "A" list. Choose only the best to be your elite Advocates. You probably only need 10 or 20 really good Advocates to build your business by referral. My suggestion is no more than 100 Advocates at any given time. Of course only you will know what the optimum number for your business is.

Let's Qualify!

Qualifying your clients for your *Referral Harvester* is absolutely crucial. You don't want to waste time and energy on someone who has no potential for sending referrals your way. Everyone is different. Some people will understand the concept of referrals and others won't – that's life, accept it and move on. When one of your clients just doesn't "get it" and you know you'll not get any referrals from him or her, it does not mean that they are bad clients. You'll still do business with them as before. They just won't form part of your *Referral Harvester*.

Remember that you effectively have two databases. One database is your normal client database which you use in the day-to-day running of your business. This database contains details of all your clients. Your second database is your *Referral Harvester*. This is the database we are working with here. This database contains details of a select group of your total client base. At this point, you have already eliminated a number of your clients from your *Referral Harvester* database. This was done in Chapter 2, when you "Deleted" some clients.

The same process will again be applied during qualification. When your qualification process eliminates a client, he or she is re-coded to "D" (delete). They still remain your client but will not form part of your *Referral Harvester* system.

The purpose of qualification is to ensure that you are spending time and energy harvesting referrals only from those clients who have the potential to give you referrals. Skipping this step can result in a waste of time, energy and money.

Referral Harvester User Comment

Colin L. is an Office Supplies Distributor based in Scotland.

"Years ago, when I just started out in business, I made the same mistake many business owners make today – I tried to build relationships with every single one of my clients. I believed I could obtain referrals from all my clients if I just worked harder at building those relationships. With the high volume of clients I had at the time, this soon became impossible – and quite costly. I would spend a few hours each day on the phone with clients or having face-to-face meetings and then have to work longer hours just to get the business of the day done.

I then learned the magic of qualifying clients and how important this step is in building a Referral Harvester. At first it was very difficult – how can I 'Delete' this client? I felt a bit guilty for leaving some clients out of my Referral Harvester, because they were good clients and often friends too. I learned however, that by qualifying my clients, I could save time and energy which could then be spent on the select few who would provide me with more business – over and over again."

Using a survey to qualify your clients

Experience indicates that a survey is the best and easiest way to qualify your clients for the purposes of creating a *Referral Harvester*. A survey serves a very important secondary purpose as well. The secondary purpose is getting feedback from your clients on a number of issues ranging from product quality to customer service experience. Your clients have the opportunity to tell you how to improve your products, product ranges, sales process and their overall experience in dealing with your company. Giving them this opportunity sends a clear message that you value your clients and that their input is important to you.

Apart from this secondary purpose a survey provides, it is also a very useful tool to qualify clients for your *Referral Harvester*. Running a survey can take the form of a telephone conversation or a web-based form, which your clients can complete. You will know which method will work best for your customers / clients.

Referral Harvester User Comment

Joanne D. is a Marketing Consultant and Content Marketing Specialist, based in the UK.

"It's easy to undervalue the impact we have on our clients' businesses so sometimes it's not until we receive their survey back that we appreciate how they really feel about us. Until then, I hadn't asked clients for feedback and had left it to chance. Receiving feedback has actually made me more confident about the work I do, more open when receiving

feedback and keen to improve what I do based on constructive criticism.

The comments section of my client care survey has generated a great number of positive, informative statements from clients that I can use in my own marketing materials and on my website. Prospective clients will be looking for affirmation when choosing who they want to work with and a client's description of their positive experience or the impact on their business is more powerful than anything I can say to them."

Telephone survey

When conducting a survey via telephone, a few important points need to be considered:

- Keep it short – less than 4 minutes
- Make it easy
- Ensure that it is a convenient time
- Caller and salesperson should not be the same person

Your client probably does not have the time for a long-winded survey. Neither does your caller. You need to keep the survey short, with a maximum of five questions to be answered by your client. Completing the survey should be made easy. Just as they won't have a great deal of time to spend on completing your survey, they also don't want to struggle through a difficult exercise. Use questions with a choice of scaled answers. This gives your client the option to choose how happy they were with your service. Examples of questions will follow later in the chapter.

It is crucial that your caller checks with the client if the timing of the call is convenient. If not, schedule a more appropriate time. Catching your client at an inconvenient time and not being sensitive to this fact, will negatively impact on the survey and on your business. This is to be avoided at all costs.

One of the purposes of the survey is to obtain genuine feedback from your client. He or she needs to know that they can speak freely and give you their honest opinion. For this reason it is important to have someone else, other than the salesperson, make this call to your client. If you work alone and are not only the salesperson but also the cleaner, admin clerk and the tea-maker, you need to find a friend or family member to conduct your survey calls. The client will feel more comfortable to give honest feedback if they speak to someone other than the salesperson they dealt with originally.

Web-based survey

Surveys set up online can save a great deal of time, are cost effective and less intrusive than a survey via telephone. Once the survey has been set up, it can be used over and over again by all your clients. After successfully setting up the survey, you only need to send the link to your clients via e-mail (included in a personal note) and the job is basically done. This saves time and effort on your part. A web-based survey is a cost-effective way to qualify your clients for your *Referral Harvester*. You can add a survey page to your website which is not visible to the general public but can be accessed via a link sent to clients. There are also many free surveys online which you can use. Do a quick search online to find relevant sites or choose the best one for you from the list below. This is by no means an exhaustive list:

- www.surveymonkey.com
- www.quicksurveys.com

- www.freeonlinesurveys.com
- www.kwiksurveys.com
- www.questionpro.com
- www.websurveycreator.com
- www.smart-survey.co.uk

It is important to remember to include a field in your survey, where your client should insert their name or e-mail address. Without this information, it would be impossible to determine which answers came from which client. Proper qualification and follow-up requires you to know what information and feedback each client provided.

Another benefit of the online survey is the fact that it is not intrusive. Your client will receive an e-mail from you with a link to the survey. He or she can then complete the survey at a convenient time. Your client might also feel more relaxed while completing the survey as they are taking this action when and where it suits them, which might result in more thought going into each answer. You can then collect and analyse the data.

Referral Harvester User Comment

Pete G. and Andrew P. are international Marketing Consultants based in the UK.

"Survey Monkey is a great tool for this, we edited our DNS Settings in our domain name so feedback.XXX.com linked to our survey – which made it really easy to send out our survey and it looked professional. We simply incorporated this into our customer care cycle, we already asked clients for feedback, so in the same survey we asked the question: 'In the future, how likely is it that you would recommend us to a friend?' The answer to this question helped coding our clients. As a bonus question we asked 'Is there anybody you have in mind that

could use our services at the moment, if so – we'll give them a 10% discount since they have been introduced through you.'

Referral Harvester User Comment

Heather W. is an Event Consultant and Manager, based in the UK.

"I have used online surveys so as people can do it when they have enough time. Giving the information of how long it will take them e.g. 4 minutes, and also limiting the number of questions to 5, has certainly increased the number of responses.

By saying at the end of the survey that I would like to connect on LinkedIn, has increased my recommendations on LinkedIn too!"

Survey questions

A MUST question in your survey deals with qualifying your client – this is after-all the main purpose of the survey. This question should ask the client how likely they are to refer you to friends, family and other contacts. The survey can be created to provide scaled options for each answer. For example, five numbered options with "Very Likely", being 5 on the scale and "Not at all" being 1 on the scale. The client can then choose how likely they are to refer their contacts to you.

Your survey can further include questions aimed at getting feedback regarding your products and client service. Examples of these types of questions can be found below.

- How would you rate the manner in which the salesperson dealt with your transaction?

- How would you rate the value for money factor during your recent transaction?
- On a scale of 1 to 5, with 5 being highest, how would you rate the quality of our product / service?
- On a scale of 1 to 5, with 5 being highest, how promptly was your query dealt with?

You can also add a text block at the end of your survey where clients can leave comments. This will provide a platform for your clients to voice opinions not covered in the questions or to further explain certain points. A text block like this gives you very specific feedback and can also result in great testimonials from clients, or a criticism that might alert you to a potential problem.

Referral Harvester User Comment

Jacqui L. an Accountant based in North London uses a web-based survey in her accountancy business.

"I have never felt comfortable asking clients for testimonials. When I started using a survey to qualify my clients, I discovered the added advantage of getting testimonials without asking! A number of my clients have used the text box in my survey to write really nice things about me and the service I provide. These I now use in other marketing material. Bonus!"

Referral Harvester User Comment

Beverly S. is an Organisation Development Consultant based in the UK.

"Since attending the Referral Harvester course I have changed my approach to obtaining feedback and seek to categorise people from the feedback I receive. I have included two direct questions surrounding being recommended to others. I ask if

they would recommend the course to others. I also ask if they would recommend my company to others. Both questions are on a sliding scale 1-6."

Action Time

Taking into account issues such as volume of clients, time availability, cost and convenience – decide which type of survey will work best for you and your business.

- Make notes of the main points you would like covered in the survey
- Structure your questions in easy language
- If using a telephone survey, type your questions in script form
- If using a web-based survey, find the best site to use and build your survey

Image 2 is an example of an online survey.

1) What is your E-mail address?

2) How would you rate the following:

	Terrible	Poor	Good	Very Good	Excellent
Workbook	○	○	○	○	○
Venue	○	○	○	○	○
Presentation	○	○	○	○	○
Content	○	○	○	○	○

3) How can we improve the workshop?

4) How likely are you to recommend this workshop to your contacts?

Never	Not Likely	Maybe	Likely	Very Likely
○	○	○	○	○

5) Any other comments or feedback?

Ready, get set, go!

Once your survey is constructed, you can use it over and over again. You might find over time, you want to change a question or two or just restructure here and there. This is easy to do whether you use a telephone survey or a web-based survey. In fact, making slight changes in your survey from time to time is a good thing. It shows that you are taking on board the opinions of your clients and honing the survey to give you the best results. Take a fresh look at your survey every few months to determine how you can improve it.

Action Time

It is now time for implementation. Systematically work through your Funnel spreadsheet, conducting the survey with each client on the list. Start with all the "C" group clients as they are the latest additions to the list. Then survey all your "B" group clients. Even though your "A" group clients are already advocating you and your business, it is a good idea to survey them as well. It will re-enforce their belief that you value their opinion and you will get good, honest feedback.

While conducting your survey, try to make it a little personal. Make your client feel that you are speaking to them personally and not just blanket surveying clients (you are indeed doing a blanket survey, but the client still needs to feel they are special). Use the client's name when speaking to him or her, but don't overuse a name – that sounds too scripted. The other ace up your sleeve is the last transaction date. Looking at your Funnel spreadsheet, you'll find the last date you did business with this client. During the conversation or typed into the e-mail, refer to this date of last transaction. This tells your client that you are on top of everything happening in your business and that your systems are functioning perfectly. You know all about their last transaction – you just want their opinion on the experience.

Image 3 is an example of this type of E-mail.

Hi Paul
First of all, I would like to thank you for attending the Referral Harvester Workshop! Your input, feedback and observations on the day were invaluable to me and I greatly appreciate it. My hope is that the Referral Harvester system will become a very successful part of your marketing strategy – please keep me posted!

I firmly believe in continual improvement. In order to evolve Talking Business Limited into the absolute best business of its kind, I need your feedback with regards to the Referral Harvester Workshop you completed on 11 June 2015. Please could you spare five minutes to complete my survey.

Survey Link: www.testsurvey.com

Thank you in advance for completing my survey – much appreciated.

And the results are in...

As the results of your survey are collected, you need to capture the data in your Funnel spreadsheet. You will use the "Notes" column for this purpose. As the main purpose of the survey is to determine their willingness to refer you to their contacts, you will focus mostly on the question relevant to this particular issue. All other information gathered regarding product quality, service and value for money can be analysed separately to gain an understanding of potential improvement in the day-to-day running of your business.

Your clients will answer with a 1, 2, 3, 4 or 5 on the scale in the question regarding their willingness to tell their contacts about you and your business. These numbers will represent their opinions as explained below.

1. Never
2. I don't think I would
3. Maybe
4. Probably
5. Definitely

Those clients answering with a 1 or a 2 need further analysis. In the "Notes" field of your Funnel spreadsheet, type the relevant number and make a note to refer this client to your customer service team. It is obvious from their response that these clients were not very happy with some aspect of their transaction with you. You or your team can analyse the complete survey result of each of these clients and then take the appropriate action, as you would normally do within your business. At this point, these clients will not continue along the journey of becoming part of your *Referral Harvester*. They might become part of the "D" group (Delete) or, after positive action by your customer service team, they might be moved up to the "B" group. Until a result is clear, after intervention from your customer service team, these clients remain in the "C" group with a note in the "Notes" field.

Clients who answered with a 3, 4 or 5 clearly have potential to become part of your *Referral Harvester*. The relevant number should be typed into the "Notes" field of your Funnel spreadsheet for each client and they should be re-coded to "B". These clients will all receive education regarding you, your business and how you grow your business with your *Referral Harvester*. The education process will be covered in Chapter 4.

Action Time

Gather all the results from your survey and update each client's information in your Funnel spreadsheet. Re-code all relevant clients to "B" if they need further education. Remember, these are the clients who gave a rating of 3, 4 or 5. If a client made an additional comment in the survey, note this in the "Notes" field along with the rating.

Those clients remaining in the "C" group, with a note in the "Notes" field have to be referred to your customer service team. Make a note of the date referred to the team. Remember, these are the clients who gave a 1 or 2 rating in your survey.

Funnel example

Using the same example Funnel spreadsheet we used earlier in this chapter, and updating it after the last Action Time, your Funnel spreadsheet will now look similar to the example in Image 4 below.

Name	Code	Contact Details	Last Contact	Referral Given	Notes
Anton Jackson	B	XXX	4 Feb		4 – "Couldn't find it cheaper anywhere else"
Raz Kohli	B	XXX	7 Feb		3
Anne Rompford	A	XXX	20 Feb	Peter Andrews	5 – "Brilliant Service"
Peter Andrews	C	XXX	6 Mar		2 – 10th March – Referred to team
Lynda Smith	B	XXX	7 Mar		3

In the above example, the first client gave a rating of 4 with a comment. This has been added to the "Notes" field. His code remains "B" as he will now receive further education.

The second client gave a rating of 3 in the survey and his code remains the same. Anne, the third client, was already an advocate so her code remains the same for the moment. Her rating and comment is typed into the "Notes" field. Peter gave a rating of 2. His survey is passed to the customer service team along with his survey results, for further investigation. His code remains "C" until a result can be obtained after further investigation. Our last client, Lynda, gave a rating of 3 and her code is thus upgraded to "B" from "C". She might become an Advocate after education.

Going forward – each new client goes into the funnel

Your Funnel spreadsheet is a living document – it should be updated regularly. Each new client should be added with a "C" code, after the transaction. Depending on the volume of clients you deal with, you need to determine how often you need to update the Funnel. This should be done at least once a week – more regularly if possible.

When adding new clients to your Funnel, you also need to follow up on the "old C's". These are the clients who gave low ratings in the survey and whom you have passed along to your customer service team. They need to be re-coded, as soon as a result is obtained from your team. They either become "B" clients – thus moving along to receive further education, or they become part of the "D" group.

Those clients in the "A" and "B" groups now need further education....

Chapter 4

Educate Your Clients

You want to do business differently. Set yourself apart from the pack. You want to stand head and shoulders above your competitors – that is why you are reading (and hopefully, implementing) this book. Using your *Referral Harvester* is doing exactly that – making you stand out from the crowd. You prefer to spend your time giving fantastic service to your clients and building strong, lasting relationships with them. This is a special way of running a business – it is very different from what most business owners (and possibly, your competitors) are doing.

The thing is, YOU know you are running your business in this manner and your team or family might know you are running your business by referrals – but your CLIENTS don't know this very important fact.....yet. They won't know about your *Referral Harvester* unless you tell them. YOU need to educate your clients – tell them that you do business differently – *you gain new business by referral.*

Enter the Client Multiplier Conversation. This is a conversation you need to have with each and every client in your Funnel spreadsheet. Using this conversation, you will educate your clients into understanding how important referrals are to you. This is also the first step towards building solid relationships with your clients. During this conversation, you have the opportunity to learn a bit more about your client, educate your client, set yourself apart from your competitors and lay the foundation for harvesting referrals.

Referral Harvester User Comment

Beverly S. is an Organisation Development Consultant based in the UK.

"Personally I think building effective relationships are key. Trust is ultimately important to me. Therefore I like to build relationships that allow me to understand what the other person does and for them to understand what I do, but importantly how we work. Reputation is important. I want to make sure that the person promoting me fits with my values, quality and the industries I work in and that I match them too. I believe we can only do this by establishing a good relationship and rapport."

The Client Multiplier Conversation

The Client Multiplier Conversation has six phases, each designed to accomplish a specific goal. The six goals are:

- Learning about your client
- Introduction to education
- How your industry works
- How you work
- What you ask of them
- How this benefits them

Six goals for one, short conversation might seem a bit much but bear in mind that all the goals are interlinked to create one larger goal – educating your client.

Phase one – Learn more about your client

During the first few minutes of the Client Multiplier Conversation, you need to build rapport and get to know your client a bit better. Spend a few minutes just chatting, creating a relaxed, friendly conversation. To guide you along your way during this first phase, here are a few ideas:

- Refer to his last transaction with you – confirm that he is happy with the product
- Thank her for completing your survey
- Ask how business is going – find out about any new projects your client is working on
- Find out about your client's social media involvement – can you connect on Twitter, LinkedIn, Facebook or any other platform? Do they have a blog?

The purpose of Phase One is to serve as an ice-breaker and to gain an insight into your client, his or her business and lay the foundation for a solid relationship.

Phase two – Introduction to education

In the second part of the conversation, you start to guide the conversation towards educating your client. Examples of phrases to use in this part of the conversation are:

- "When you completed my survey, you indicated your willingness to refer your contacts to me. I really appreciate that. I would like to take this opportunity to explain to you, in more detail, how I run my business."
- "From our conversation thus far, it seems we have a similar business ethos. It is important to me that you understand how I run my business."

- "You indicated in our survey that you would be happy to refer business to us – thank you so much for that. This is a very important part of our business and I would like to explain this in more detail now."
- "From what you are saying it is clear we both want a long-term business relationship. It is therefore important to me that you understand how I run my business."

After creating a friendly, relaxed tone during Phase One, this phase brings the conversation to a more serious note. You still have the rapport and friendliness which you established earlier but now you are indicating that you want to bring across a very important point. Your client is now ready to hear all about how you run your business.

Phase three – How your industry works

During the third phase of your Client Multiplier Conversation, you need to spend a minute or two describing what other businesses in your industry are doing with regards to marketing and promotion. This will show your client that you have an awareness of your competitors' methods and will re-affirm what he or she probably already knows about your industry. Before doing business with you, they probably did a bit of research and took note of advertisements, websites and other marketing methods employed by other businesses in your industry. You are thus telling him/her what they already know but this creates a sense of agreement between the two of you. Also, it sets the stage for the next phase – by stating all of the usual marketing methods, an expectation is created that you are different from the pack. Your client is now eager to hear how you are different.

Typical dialogue during this phase is:

- "The majority of people in this industry spend their time and money on finding new clients. They do things like door knocking, cold calling, leaflet drops and advertising."
- "Most accountants spend all their marketing resources on print advertising and business exhibitions to find new prospects."
- "I'm sure you've noticed that other web developers in the area engage in a great deal of social media, leaflet drops and direct mail to find new business."

Do some research into the marketing strategies used by your competitors in your field. You need to speak from a solid knowledge base during the Client Multiplier Conversation.

Phase four – How you work

This is the main crunch of the conversation. This is where you educate your client. Now, you have the chance to distinguish yourself from everyone else. During this phase, you tell your client that you **gain new business through referrals**. Examples of dialogue in this phase are below.

- "I prefer not to spend as much time and resources on the methods I've just described. I build my business exclusively by referral and devote myself to serving my clients and their needs – not only before and during the transaction, but also long thereafter."
- "I don't do any of that. What is important to me is building solid, long-term relationships with my clients and gaining new business through referrals"
- "I choose to spend my time building great relationships with my clients. This results in a higher

quality of service to my clients as well as referrals from those clients. The core of my business is referrals."

Phase five – What you ask of them

At this point in the conversation, your client should understand that you are different from most other business owners and that you build your business on referrals. Their education should now be expanded to include where they fit into the picture. You need to explain what you expect of them. During this phase, you can use phrases such as those below.

- "I would appreciate it if you could refer any of your contacts to me, who you believe could benefit from my services."
- "All I ask is that you refer me to any of your contacts who are thinking about having their insurance reviewed and would appreciate the same level of service you have experienced with me."
- "I know you are an active networker and would greatly appreciate it if you could refer me to anyone in your network who might need a house cleaning service."

Phase six – How this benefits them

This is the final phase of the Client Multiplier Conversation. It is now time to explain the benefits to them, of your *Referral Harvester*. It is clear what the benefits to you are, and even though people like to help others, they like to know that there is something in it for them too. Below are a few examples of dialogue during the final phase of your conversation.

- "I'm sure you understand that, as long as you and my other clients keep referring me, I don't have to

go prospecting like everyone else. This means I have more time to spend on giving you the excellent service you deserve."
- "You see, by building my business on referrals, I can save time and resources which I would otherwise have to spend on finding new clients. This enables me to use that time and resources to give you and all my other clients the kind of service I believe you deserve."
- "As long as you and my other clients keep referring me, I can spend more time on building a relationship with you and learning more about your needs as a client. This allows me the opportunity to deliver an even higher standard of service to you. Does that make sense?"

This ten to fifteen minute conversation is the core of your *Referral Harvester*. By the end of the Client Multiplier Conversation your client knows you are building your business through referrals, they know why you are doing that and they know what is expected of them.

Referral Harvester User Comment

Richard F. a Builder in the North West of England was amazed by the results of a few conversations.

"When I started using the Client Multiplier Conversation, it took me nearly four weeks of phone calls to work through all my clients. Before I even reached the end of my client list, the referrals started coming in from those I had called before. Quite astonishing!

At first, it felt a bit unnatural to make the calls, but after a few calls, I started to enjoy it. In fact, making those calls was an eye-opener. I learned so much about some of my clients and in many cases we have really built a great relationship. I even found that I shared other interests and hobbies with some of them!"

Action Time

Type up a one-page "script" with guidelines you can use when having your Client Multiplier Conversation with clients. Use language that comes naturally to you – you need to sound **real**. Always, always speak in your own voice. Don't use scripted language which doesn't fit with your natural way of speaking.

Work your way through your Funnel spreadsheet, having a conversation with each of your clients. Start with your advocates – the "A" group – as they have already referred new clients to you and will thus easily understand your point. You can then work your way through the "B" group. People in your "C" group will not get this call yet. They first need to be qualified (see Chapter 3).

Re-code when necessary

From time to time, you will encounter a client who just doesn't "get it". Even though they have indicated in your survey that they would be willing to refer their contacts to you, you might get a feeling during the conversation that they are "back-peddling". Trust your gut – if you feel a resistance and you can't overcome it during the conversation, you might have to re-code that particular client. In a case like this, re-code him or her to "D" (see Chapter 2 for coding of clients).

You have sorted your database and qualified and educated each client. Now it is time to start implementing your *Referral Harvester* system...

Chapter 5

Your Referral Harvester System is Based on The Personal Touch

The *Referral Harvester* system is the successful fusion between TOMA (top of mind awareness) and the Sumimasen Philosophy. These are two very powerful concepts and having them work in partnership creates a solid client care system in your business AND ensures continuous referrals flowing in.

Top of mind awareness

TOMA results in an automatic response – when you have gained TOMA with anyone, your name will automatically pop into their minds, the moment anyone mentions your industry.

Examples:

- You are having coffee with friends at a café on a Saturday afternoon. One friend mentions they might be looking to buy a bigger house. Automatically, the name of your mortgage advisor pops into your

head – and you recommend him / her right there on the spot.
- Two business partners have a meeting with their bank manager. He knows they are involved in the property investment world (not related to their current business). He tells them that he needs to re-do the kitchen of his mother's house, which they now plan to rent out. Immediately, one of the partners asks him who he has in mind to do the actual work and he answers he doesn't have anyone yet. She whips out her phone and gives him the number of a fantastic joiner, whom they trust and hold in high regard. Just like that – referral done.
- At a business networking event, a man mentions that his car is out of action. He needs the car to be repaired urgently but his mechanic is away on holiday. He was never that satisfied with the auto repair man anyway. Another businessman overhears the conversation and offers to put him in touch with his own mechanic, who has always given him excellent service. Referral done.

That is top of mind awareness.

In order to achieve top of mind awareness with your clients, you need to implement the "drip-effect". Drip feed him / her through contact on a regular basis to remain at the forefront of their thoughts.

Referral Harvester User Comment

Heather W. is an Event Consultant and Manager, based in the UK.

"What I have found especially useful is having a private Twitter list of my A's. It means I can go in and see what they are up

to and interact with them on a regular basis. It also keeps me in their Top of Mind."

The Sumimasen Philosophy

Have you ever heard the word "sumimasen"? It is the Japanese word for "thank you" and means "this will not end".

The Sumimasen Philosophy can be explained as a form of social obligation or reciprocity. In other words, if you perform a favour for someone, they will feel a sense of future obligation towards you. Reciprocity almost always works because we are taught from a young age to return favours, and to disregard this teaching will lead to a break with our core values. The Sumimasen Philosophy has been hard-wired into our brain, without us even being consciously aware of it. It is like flying on autopilot: Someone gives you an unexpected gift and you automatically want to give them something in return.

Here are a few examples of the Sumimasen Philosophy in action: (See if you have experienced any of them)

- The waitress gives you a smile and chats away in a very friendly manner while taking your order. When delivering your order, she gives you another smile and wishes you an enjoyable meal. Subconsciously you feel great and ultimately tip the waitress slightly more than you would normally have done.
- Friends of friends invite you to dinner. You don't know them very well but accept the invitation anyway. Afterwards you feel obliged to invite them for dinner in return.
- A charity sends you a small gift of flower seeds in the mail, accompanied by a note along the lines of "spread the happiness of Spring around". Also in the

envelope, is a request for a small donation. You feel extra charitable (they have given you something of value, after all) and send off a cheque.
- You receive a Christmas card from an acquaintance, two weeks before Christmas day. You were not planning on sending out any cards this year, but now you suddenly feel that you need to send a card to this person.

You can see from these examples that saying thank you – Sumimasen "this will not end" - is by no means the end of any favour or gift received. We feel an automatic obligation to the gift giver and want to return the favour as soon as possible.

Applying the Sumimasen Philosophy in your business is easy. Your clients have already been hard-wired to respond positively upon receiving a gift or favour. The only thing left for you to do, is to give the client valuable items – in a systematic way.

Create the fusion

Neither Sumimasen nor TOMA are new concepts – we have all received a promotional item in a goody bag at a business show. But does that make you want to do business with that company? No....just a free pen isn't going to sway you to a new accountant. And the thing with TOMA is that people have been getting it wrong – they think blasting e-mails, offers and newsletters at you will create top of mind awareness. It doesn't –it creates annoyance and a quick smack of the "delete" button!

To successfully use these two concepts in your business, there needs to be a successful fusion between Sumimasen and TOMA – that is your *Referral Harvester*.

Bringing about a successful fusion of the Sumimasen Philosophy and top of mind awareness, we need to ***provide perceived value*** and ***remain in contact*** on a regular basis.

Faceless society

As I've mentioned earlier, in our electronic world, the personal touch has all but disappeared. Most businesses flood their clients with "special offer" emails, Tweets or newsletters and believe they are staying in touch with their clients. This is not the case. The majority of the world's population has already zoned out of such communications. We get a tsunami of messages every day (e-mails, Tweets, TV ads, leaflets, etc.) and the noise has reached a crescendo. We have switched off. We no longer take notice.

Stand out from the crowd

If you want your business to stand out in this immense noise, you'll need to do things differently. It is time to bring back the personal touch. It is time we really connect with our clients again and forge solid, real relationships. Relationships that will ensure not only client retention but bring about Advocates – clients who shout from the rooftops how great you, your business and your offerings are.

And now you are ready to throw this book in the bin. You are thinking "Where must I find the time to build these solid relationships with each of my clients?!" And my answer is this: It is much easier and less time consuming than you can possibly imagine.

Bridging the gap between personal and systematic

I know it is difficult to bring the words "systematic" and "authentic, personal, real relationships" into the same sentence. Our minds cannot bring these two seemingly opposite concepts together. "Systematic" seems cold and calculated while "authentic, personal, real relationships" sounds warm and....well personal.

The thing is this: doing something systematically only means you are taking actions according to a plan, with a goal in mind. It is like having reminders set up in your smartphone so you don't forget your partner's birthday or your anniversary. You have a system to help you take a personal, real and authentic action. The *Referral Harvester* works in exactly the same way.

Use a CRM (Customer Relationship Management) system

It is important to keep notes of each interaction with an Advocate. You could note personal facts, what projects they are working on, when their birthday is, when they are going on holiday and where....the list is endless. The important thing is to keep notes of it all. This is how you will be building that solid relationship. And let's face it; none of us can remember every little thing about each client! Unless you're a genius...

Action Time

Find a CRM (Customer Relationship Management) system you could use with ease. There are many free and low-cost applications available online. Do a search and find one which at least offers the following:

- Contact name and other details
- A reminder functionality
- A big notes field
- Custom fields can be created

Now populate your CRM system with your Advocate's details. You should now have an easy to use database (separate from your normal client database) where your elite Advocates reside. Only your "A" clients and "B's" who have been educated will live in your CRM system. All other clients (C's and D's) haven't made it to this elite home. This CRM system is for your *Referral Harvester* people only.

The fundamentals of the Referral Harvester System

Experience has shown that each Advocate needs 12 "touches" per annum. This provides the perfect "drip-effect" creating top of mind awareness in the minds of your Advocates. And as we have discovered earlier, top of mind awareness is one of the key ingredients of your *Referral Harvester* system.

Bear in mind that you will only have "A" and "B" coded clients in your *Referral Harvester* – not *all* your clients. You cannot build solid, authentic relationships with everybody – accept that fact. Focus only on those clients who are already Advocates and those who might become Advocates and have been educated. Do not waste time with those clients who did not meet the criteria of the *Referral Harvester*. This might sound harsh but we have to face facts and focus our energy on those clients who will bring us referrals. Remember, all your clients will still experience your outstanding client service. It is just your Advocates and would-be Advocates who belong to an elite club – your *Referral Harvester*.

So it is these clients – the ones in your *Referral Harvester* elite club – who will receive 12 "touches" each year.

But, as I tried to make clear earlier in this chapter, adding your client to your newsletter mailing list just won't do. These 12 "touches" need to be much more personal. And varied. Making an obligatory phone call every month to a client won't work either. We need more than that. We need to stand out from the crowd. We need to build real, authentic relationships in order to power-up the force of the Sumimasen Philosophy.

The Referral Harvester system is designed to provide those 12 "touches" in a varied way throughout the year. The "touches" create top of mind awareness (by making regular contact) and leverage the power of the Sumimasen Philosophy through the types of "touches" you will be making.

Referral Harvester User Comment

Pete G. and Andrew P. are international Marketing Consultants based in the UK.

"The results of keeping top of mind awareness are phenomenal, even just little things like sending a postcard after work has been completed just to say thanks can melt the clients' hearts and turn them into passionate brand advocates. Not to mention some of our clients still have our quirky postcards on their board even years later!"

Types of touches

In the following chapters we will look at each type of "touch" individually with examples of what you can implement in your own *Referral Harvester*. I want to add a note here - please be creative. Think out of the box. Make each "touch" as personal as you can. The "touches" which will form part of your *Referral Harvester* are:

- Valuable Items (VIs)
- Phone / Skype / E-mail
- Personal Notes
- Drop-by / Meet up
- Gift

There are no set rules as to how many of each type of "touches" you need to make with each client, over the period of a year. It is however important to include all these "touches" as it creates the sense of obligation which is a vital part of your *Referral Harvester*. It is also important to vary the types of "touches" or else things might become a bit predictable and downright boring. Make it fun; make it something your Advocate (and you) looks forward to. As a guide, you could send four Valuable Items, make three phone / skype / email contacts, send two personal notes, have two drop-by / meet ups and give one gift. As the year comes to an end, you can merely repeat the process again for the next year.

Let's look at what I mean by Valuable Items in the next chapter.

Chapter 6

Valuable Item: Leveraging the Sumimasen Philosophy

As explained in Chapter 5, during the next year, you will be sending three to four Valuable Items to each Advocate and would-be Advocate. This not only serves to remind them of you and your business, but it also harnesses the power of the Sumimasen Philosophy. After receiving the first Valuable Item, a subconscious sense of obligation will start to form in the mind of your client. Further Valuable Items, used in conjunction with calls, e-mails, personal notes etc. will only increase the feeling of indebtedness your client feels towards you.

People are all different. One client might start to respond positively after just one or two interactions – others might take a little longer.

Referral Harvester User Comment

Kate M. is a Healthcare Consultant based in the UK.

"I loved this as it provides a way of connecting with clients regularly without feeling like you are pestering them or feeling false. And being on the receiving end is fantastic! I love it when one of your 'touches' comes through my door as I instantly think of you and your business. It makes me feel valued."

What is a Valuable Item: Time to think out of the box

You don't need to break the bank. The value in any item is in fact *perceived value*. What will your clients perceive as a valuable item? The act of giving a Valuable Item is much more about what the recipient feels upon receipt, than about what the item cost you. Value, in this case, can be measured in emotional currency rather than monetary currency. You want to create a situation where your client thinks: "How nice of Louise to have thought of me". You do not want a situation where your client thinks: "My goodness, this must have cost quite a bit. Ahmed must be making so much money that he doesn't need any more business".

When choosing Valuable Items, keep the following pointers in mind:

- The emotional value should be higher than the monetary value
- Make the recipient feel "special" – as if this item will make a difference in their own lives, however small that difference is
- Give the recipient something to talk about to friends and family
- It should not be so costly as to negatively affect your business
- It should be small in size, to make it easier to mail to your client if needed

- Digital *and* physical items can be valuable
- Valuable Items can be chosen with a client's personal interests in mind

Different types of Valuable Items

You might want to give Valuable Items that are very industry specific. For example, in the case of a B2B (business to business) construction material company, most of their clients are other construction companies, so most of their Valuable Items could centre around the construction industry. One type of Valuable Item they could use would be news articles about the latest developments in the industry. Alternatively, you could choose items that are more personal to the client, or a mix of personal and professionally themed items. Bear in mind that you will be giving each client three to four Valuable Items over the course of 12 months. A variety would be a good idea.

Informative news articles

There is no shortage of news articles in the world today. You can find these in magazines, newspapers, online on many different types of websites as well as on social media sites. If you subscribe to industry specific publications, and you think your clients can benefit from a specific article, send it off to them as a Valuable Item. The same is true for information on blogs, news websites or online forums specialising in your industry. Giving information that is industry specific as a Valuable Item solidifies the perception that you are on top of the latest developments in your industry.

Giving information of a more personal nature creates a stronger emotional reaction. It makes your client feel that you are thinking of them personally. If you know your client loves playing golf, and you come across an article about the latest design in golf clubs, send the article to that client. This will show your client that you are interested in him or her personally, and that it is not just all about business. Another example is sending a new cake recipe you have found on a blog to a client whom you know loves cooking and baking. Send a short note with the link, in an e-mail.

Promotional items

Giving your client a promotional item has a double benefit. Firstly, your client perceives it as something useful (and therefore valuable) and secondly, it is advertising for you and your business. Following are a few factors to consider when deciding on what type of promotional item to use:

- It needs to be cost effective
- The item should be small enough to be mailed to a client
- Think of the longevity of the item – how long would it last before it gets binned?
- It should be large enough to contain all relevant information – your name, company name, contact details and - if your company name does not make it clear - your industry (or what you do)
- The item should be different from the normal, run-of-the-mill promotional items. Think of something new and exciting – think out of the box

You can do research online to get ideas of available promotional items. You can also contact promotional item providers with any new ideas you might come up with – discuss your ideas with them and possibly have them create a new range for you. However do not feel limited to promotional item providers. If you think of a new item which is not available from standard providers, contact other, independent manufacturers and discuss your ideas with them.

Referral Harvester User Comment

Andrew B is a Real Estate Broker on the south coast in South Africa.

"I know many people give printed calendars to their clients, so I wanted to do something slightly different. I had a graphic designer create a special 'what's on' calendar and had it printed on a card. As I'm based in a relatively small town, it was easy to create a list of all the social and cultural events in our area taking place on a regular basis.

I gave each client a copy of my 'what's on' calendar and they were very well received. It works even better with people new to our area as it helps them integrate into our community. I am still providing these cards to my clients each year and it has become a bit of an institution in our area."

Company newsletter

If your company produces regular newsletters, you can use these as Valuable Items. Company newsletters often contain industry news, latest products or services, testimonials from clients, new projects and other informative tit-bits. All of this can be classed as valuable information (otherwise the newsletter is pointless, really).

Just a word of caution here: Do not fall into the "easy road trap". Some people have made the error of adding their clients to their newsletter mailing list, thinking this covers all Valuable Items for the year – all done and dusted. Using only your company newsletter as Valuable Items will not create much of an emotional reaction from your client. Newsletters are, in general, written for the masses and not designed to make any client feel special. Your client will know that you send the newsletter to potentially thousands of people, so it is not written with them in mind. Newsletters do not really have the "personal touch" element needed in a successful referral system. That said, there is still a place for company newsletters within the Valuable Items list. The idea however is to minimise its use as a Valuable Item to a maximum of three newsletters over a two-year period.

Invitations to events

Inviting your client to an event where there is a clear benefit to attend, will be strongly perceived as valuable by your client. Not only will they have the opportunity to learn something new and make new contacts – they will also view your invitation as something special with just them in mind. Usually, it is not possible for anyone to invite hundreds of people to the same event. Your client therefore feels that they have received an exclusive and valuable item.

Many events are held all across the country every week. Finding suitable events should not pose a problem. You might be part of a local networking group where keynote speakers address various interesting topics. One or more of your clients might benefit from a discussion on these specific topics. If so, invite them along. Often one gets invited to an event and asked to bring a friend along. In such a case you can invite a client to accompany you. Searching online for local events will give you a variety of events to choose from. A few examples of suitable events follow:

- Seminars: Seminars covering topics of interest to your clients could be very beneficial to them. Topics could include anything from the latest social media strategies to fashion design.
- Workshops: If you think a client would find this useful, and be interested in attending a workshop,

invite them along. A wide variety of workshops are often available locally, including workshops on business development, self-development, crafts etc.
- Networking events: These events can benefit any of your clients running their own business and also for those in sales and marketing positions. Be careful though, as some networking groups can be aggressive in their marketing. You do not want your client to feel that you will benefit more from the invitation than they would. Make sure that there is a clear benefit to your client when sending such an invitation.
- Business exhibitions: If you and your client operate within the same industry, invitations to these events can be perfect Valuable Items. It not only has clear benefits for your client, but it also reinforces the perception that you are up to date with the latest developments in your industry.
- Company event: If you and your company are planning an event or a product launch, you could invite a few clients to attend. Ensure you spend time with each client in particular during the event. You need to make them feel that you appreciate their attendance and that they are special – not just another name on the guest list.

Website links

Adding a link to your website, pointing to the website or blog of your client, is an excellent Valuable Item. Most businesses and individuals have websites and/or blogs these days and most will appreciate incoming links. The benefit to them is clear in that it will assist with the popularity of their website or blog.

In some cases your client might benefit on another level – through added credibility. Having external links to one's website usually gives one a higher standing and credibility. This is potentially massive value you can give your client.

Testimonials and recommendations

It is widely accepted that testimonials and recommendations give more credibility to any business. If you operate within the B2B arena, these can be the "gold dust" of all Valuable Items.

Offering to write a testimonial for a client, which he or she can use on their website or any other literature, will be experienced as enormously valuable by your client. The benefit to them is immeasurable – it could lead to more business for them and would add weight to their sales-pitch.

A variation of this type of testimonial is a recommendation on social media sites such as the business orientated LinkedIn. Many people read online profiles of potential business contacts before engaging in a business transaction. If your client has a few recommendations in his or her online profile, it will lend weight to their professionalism. Your recommendation could open doors for your client, which makes this type of Valuable Item extremely valuable.

This is by no means an exhaustive list of potential Valuable Items. The list is endless as each industry and client differs. Thinking of new Valuable Items is fun and easy.

Action Time

Let's start weaving Valuable Items into your referral system. This can be accomplished with an easy two-step brainstorming session.

Valuable Items across the board

Get a pen and sheet of paper ready. You now need to identify one or two Valuable Items which you can use for all your clients. In other words, you are looking for a "one size fits all" Valuable Item. Scan through the potential Valuable Items listed in this chapter asking yourself this question: "Can I give this type of Valuable Item to each of my clients?" When you find an item on the list to which the answer is "yes", make a note of it on the sheet of paper.

Spend a bit of time thinking out of the box. Are there any other Valuable Items you can use for all of your clients which are not listed in this chapter? Add all new ideas to your list on the sheet of paper.

Your sheet of paper might now look something like the following:

- Promotional item – Branded fridge magnet / keyring / flash drive
- Company Newsletter
- Company Event
- News Article

Think about each of the items on your list and try to narrow the list down to two or three items. Things to take into account when making the final decision on the items you will use are monetary cost, time needed and ease of sending the item.

Now go back to your Funnel spreadsheet you created in Chapter 3 and make the appropriate notes next to each client's name.

Use the personal touch

The Valuable Item part of your *Referral Harvester* system is now half-way complete – well done! You now have one or two Valuable items designated for each client. You now need to find a further one or two Valuable Items, to complete this part of your *Referral Harvester* system (remember, you will be sending three or four Valuable Items to each of your clients over the next 12 months, so you now have to fill in the blanks).

It is now time to think about each client specifically. Use the list of qualified clients you created in Chapter 3. During the qualifying process, you learnt a bit about each client. Use that knowledge now to decide what type of Valuable Item you can give each client in turn. Take a sheet of paper and draw three columns. Name the columns with client name, VI 1 and VI 2. Write your client's name on the first line and then add one of two Valuable Items next to his or her name.

Your list of personal Valuable Items will now look something like Image 5.

Client Name	Valuable Item 1	Valuable Item 2
Jason	Website link	Invite to networking
Tina	Website link	Informative article
Elizabeth	Invite to networking	Recommendation on LinkedIn
Valerie	Testimonial	Music CD
Jackson	Invitation to art workshop	Art article

Now go back to your *Referral Harvester* CRM system and populate your notes field with all the Valuable Items for each of your clients, as per your decisions in this chapter. Congratulations! You now have the three to four Valuable Items to give each of your clients over the next 12 months.

Chapter 7

Using Technology and Old-Time Charm in Harmony

Don't you just love a good old chat with a friend?! Of course we all do and that is exactly what you will be doing with your Advocates. Phone / Skype calls form part of the 12 annual "touches" we make with each of our Advocates. As a guide, you need to make about three of these types of "touches" every year, with each Advocate.

The aim is not to sell

Don't you just hate those sales calls?! Of course you do – we all do. So don't morph these "touches" into sales calls. Have a conversation and don't even *think* of selling. Focus the call on your Advocate; what are they up to, how is business going (in the case of B2B), refer to a fact you talked about in an earlier conversation. This is merely a catch-up call; a type of conversation you probably have dozens of times each day with friends and colleagues. Make is personal, friendly and relaxed. At no point should your Advocate feel you have called to sell them your latest widget.

The aim is to gather information

These types of "touches" are fantastic opportunities to gather information about your client and learn more about what is important to him / her. You might find out more about their hobbies, holidays, new projects or social media habits. All of this information then gets fed into your Referral Harvester system (CRM) in order to make it easier for you to choose great Valuable Items for this particular client. It also serves as an ice-breaker during your next "touch" as you can refer back to a previous comment.

Examples:

- A few years ago, one of my Advocates mentioned that they were going on a skiing trip to the French Alps, the following month. The next "touch" I made (about a month later) was a hand-written card wishing them a fabulous holiday. (More about personal notes and cards later in this chapter).
- During a phone call with one of my Advocates, she told me about a close friend of hers who had just lost her mother after a long illness. The amazing thing is that the friend she was talking about was also one of my Advocates. Needless to say, directly after that phone call, I made a call to my other Advocate who was experiencing a family bereavement.
- How the conversation came about, I still don't know (bearing in mind this is a B2B situation) but an Advocate mentioned that she is a mad knitter who belongs to a knitting club and knits all kinds of things all the time. It just so happened that I noticed the cutest knitted slippers in my Facebook feed a few weeks later. The post gave information about where to find the knitting pattern for these slippers.

Guess what I did? Yes, I sent her the link – Valuable Item done for the next month.

One thing to keep in mind though is not to interrogate. This is a friendly conversation between two people building a relationship; not the Spanish Inquisition. Just let it flow naturally without focusing too much on gathering as much information as possible. You don't want to sound too nosey, after all. And a call doesn't have to take up too much time either. A ten-minute conversation will serve your purpose perfectly.

Don't you just love a card?

The wonderful thing about a hand-written card is that people find it really difficult to throw away. Cards are kept; on the notice board, fridge, mantle-piece and window sills. The longevity of this type of "touch" is remarkable. And that is exactly what we are aiming for here. Top of mind awareness. With your card living in your Advocate's space for any period of time, you are assured that they will have you top of mind.

I have a large pin-board on my office wall. Most of it is covered in cards I have received from clients. I just can't bring myself to bin any of them. I have an emotional attachment to each of those cards – each one reminds me of a specific person and/or memory. And I'm certainly not the only one with the habit of keeping cards. Most people, including your Advocates, keep cards for a least a little while. Leverage that habit. Send at least two hand-written cards or notes to each Advocate each year.

The types of cards you use are really up to you. Make it something that will resonate with your client and represent you – in an authentic, true and real manner. I am often asked what should be written in the card to a client. This again, is entirely up to you but here are a few examples:

- Birthday cards
- Write an inspirational quote that made you think of this client
- Thank them for their continued support
- Wish them a relaxing holiday
- Tell them about an upcoming event they might be interested in

You can choose to bulk-buy cards or find those little personal, hand-made cards for your clients. One thing I would advise though is to make a note of the type of card you send to the client, in your CRM system. You don't want to send the same card to the same person twice!

Referral Harvester User Comment

Craig B. is an Independent Financial Advisor, based in London.

"One of the wonderful ladies in my A group is an art lover. During a visit to the Galleria dell'Accademia in Italy, I bought her a beautiful postcard and sent it to her upon my return to the UK. She very often gave me referrals but this particular instance is noteworthy. A friend of hers, who is also an art lover, visited her and saw my postcard on her fridge. They got talking about it which lead my Advocate to tell her friend all about me and my services. My Advocate didn't even think her friend might need my services, as they have never really discussed financial planning. However, during this conversation over my postcard, it became clear that my Advocate's friend had been thinking about obtaining financial advice. My Advocate made the referral to me right away – all because of my postcard!"

Personal notes equal the ultimate personal touch

As with hand-written cards, personal notes can have a phenomenal emotional effect on people. These are often kept as well which helps in creating top of mind awareness. Due to the personal and emotional impact, it also leverages the Sumimasen Philosophy.

Whenever you send a physical Valuable Item, always include a personal note or card. Make sure it is hand-written. I also use personal notes sometimes to thank my Advocates for referrals received. It is personal and shows you took the time to hand-write a note to them. In today's world of e-mails, personal notes and cards are rather special.

Another type of "touch" I have used in the past is this: I was on a family holiday in Australia and decided to buy typical tourist postcards for each of my Advocates. As this was a 5-week holiday, I knew I needed to make a "touch" during that time and thought a postcard would be great. I wrote a note on each card and posted it off, back home. When I returned home, every single Advocate contacted me to thank me for the postcard. They were very appreciative that I thought of them even while on holiday.

Personal notes and cards are powerful "touches". Include at least two of these into your annual *Referral Harvester*.

Chapter 8

The Magic of Face-to-Face Interaction

A great way to really connect with someone is to meet for a coffee (or whatever drink you prefer). This doesn't take a massive amount of time but the positive impact on your relationship can be incalculable.

As mentioned earlier when I covered phone calls, these face-to-face meetings should never include selling. The aim of a coffee meet is purely building your relationship with your client. Use it to find out more about the client; what they like doing in their spare time, which charities they support, which sports team they root for etc. All of this will help you to solidify the supplier-client relationship.

This is also a perfect opportunity to reinforce your Client Multiplier Conversation (see Chapter 4). Weave into your conversation how important client referrals are. Vocalise your appreciation for all the referrals you have already received from the client. Make the client feel appreciated and special. A 30-minute coffee meet is a really personal "touch" which will go a long way towards leveraging their sense of obligation and creating top of mind awareness.

Tiana Wilson-Buys

I'm in your area....

Spend a bit of time planning your week ahead. Your schedule might take you near the offices of one or more of your Advocates. If that is the case, plan a drop-by.

A drop-by is just that; it is not a scheduled meeting and should take no longer than 5 minutes. Call your advocate from the car to check if he / she is in the office. Ask if you could quickly drop by to say hello. Be clear that you do not intend to stay longer than 5 minutes. This shows respect for their time and also enforces the impression that he / she is in your thoughts.

When you arrive, take special care to follow the "drop-by rules":

- Remain standing, even if they offer you a seat (this shows you are really only staying for 5 minutes and that you are true to your word)
- Do not accept the offer of a drink or something to eat.
- Focus the conversation on the client
- Leave after 5 minutes
- Thank them for their time

Drop-bys and coffee meets are great opportunities to build on your relationship with your client. They are personal (showing that you put aside special time for them) and they have greater impact than any of the other types of "touches". As a guide, do two of this type of "touch" each year with each Advocate.

Referral Harvester User Comment

Richard F. is a Builder in the North West of England

"I love dropping by my Advocates! It sometimes happens that I'll finish a job by mid-afternoon and have an hour or two spare. It's usually silly to try and start another job then, so I'll use these hours to do drop-bys. It definitely helps to build those relationships, but I have also found that it often leads to more work from that client. When I drop by, they remember that they needed this or that done and I can book them in right then. It works a charm for me!"

Many of us have clients outside of our own geographical area. This clearly makes it more difficult if not impossible to have coffee meets or drop-bys. If you can plan a trip to their area sometime during the year, make a point to have a coffee meet with them. If this is completely impossible, I suggest you make use of Skype or any other video conferencing tool to have a special kind of coffee meet – a virtual one.

Non-systematic "Bump-Into's" – these are extra!

You might see your clients often at business networking events, seminars or industry related events. These accidental "bump-into's" should not be considered as part of your 12 annual "touches". These are extra bonus interactions which you did not plan. Obviously it helps to create top of mind awareness, but see it as an added bonus. Continue with your 12 *Referral Harvester* "touches" as per plan.

I meet many of my Advocates at business networking events on a regular basis, and these bonus meets can be used quite effectively. When I know my Advocate will be at a certain networking event, I'll call them up a week or two prior to the networking and arrange a coffee meet with them for directly after networking. This works well as it saves both of us travel time (as we are there already) and we get the opportunity to catch up.

A gift for your A-team

The final "touch" type is a gift. Personally, I give one gift per annum (maximum two). The idea behind the gift is not to spend a lot of money, but rather to put extra thought into it. Find a gift which is specially chosen for that particular client. Think about their hobbies and interests. The gift needn't be work related.

Examples:

- A box of chocolates, nuts or fruit are usually a safe bet (particularly if you do not yet know a lot about the client)
- Flowers or a plant will always do the trick
- A sales consultant I know took a small ever-green pot plant to each client near Christmas time with a little card which read: "May your sales grow and blossom in the New Year".
- A music CD can be sent via the postal service
- Sports enthusiasts could receive sporting equipment (like a golfing divot tool) or memorabilia (A high-end sales executive bought a signed rugby jersey for one of his clients).
- A business book (like this one….) can be sent via the postal service
- Tickets to an event your client would be interested in

Get creative. Make it fun. Find that special gift for your client and Advocate once a year. When you present the gift is entirely up to you. You could give gifts towards the end of the year, as the sales consultant I mentioned earlier, does. Or you could coincide your gift-giving with the client's birthday or business anniversary. Alternatively, for even greater surprise and impact, give a gift at a random time in the year.

At this point, you should understand all of the "touch" types in your *Referral Harvester*. In the next chapter we'll start implementing your newfound knowledge.

Chapter 9

Putting It All Together

I don't believe in rigid systems. We are all different and we run our businesses each in our own way. There is no one-size-fits all solution to any business issue. I have shown you, in this book, the *Referral Harvester* system. This system has been proven over time by many business men and women, in varying industries; not least by myself in my own business. But no system should be rigid and you need to mould your *Referral Harvester* to fit your own business style.

The core elements of your *Referral Harvester* system are:

- Sort your database and code each client
- Create a Funnel spreadsheet to capture all potential Advocates
- Qualify each client
- Educate your would-be Advocates
- Take specific actions at specific times to leverage your *Referral Harvester*

As long as you apply each of these core elements in your Referral Harvester, you will experience fantastic relationships with your clients and they will feed your business with referrals. Exactly how you take each action and what tools you use, is up to you.

No software – what now?

When I first designed the early version of the *Referral Harvester* system in 2006, I had no CRM system to keep on top of my Advocates. I used a simple Microsoft Word document for each Advocate. I created a little template with tables to fill in. This worked perfectly well at the time. I also didn't have access to online survey tools, so my personal assistant at the time, made phone calls to would-be Advocates to qualify them. It worked very well.

Having no clever software is no excuse not to get started. Use paper and pen if you have to. Just do it! Create your *Referral Harvester* as soon as possible and use it.

Image 6 is an extract of one of my original advocate documents. (I have removed all identifying factors, for the sake of confidentiality)

Advocate: B. H.	Tel: XXX
E-mail: XXX.XXX.co.za	Cell: XXX
Birthday: 16 Aug	1st Transaction: 8 Feb 2007
Address: XXX	

Date	Action
8 Feb 2007	Met B.H. at new property with welcome gift (pot plant)
12 Feb 2007	Called B.H. – qualify. "Yes, he's happy to recommend us." Updated spreadsheet. Educated.
15 Feb 2007	Sent PN (blue card 1)
16 Mar 2007	Sent VI (article from "Keur" about preventing knee problems for marathon runners)
22 Mar 2007	Received referral of J. M. – she wants to buy a small house. She is the cousin of B.H. Thanked him via phone and e-mail.
13 Apr 2007	Called B.H. – he is preparing for "Die Voet" marathon. Planning to re-do kitchen soon.
17 May 2007	Sent PN – (ocean card) to wish him luck with "die Voet".
28 May 2007	Received referral of J. L. R. – ran "die Voet" with B.H. – he is looking for residential land on the hill. Thanked B.H. via phone and e-mail.
15 June 2007	Meet-up with B.H. at XXX Coffee Shoppe – new kitchen being installed next week. He applied for a promotion – will know by mid of July. Going on holiday to XXX in Sep.
16 July 2007	Called B.H. – wished him luck with promotion.

Let's run through this old Advocate Document to create a better understanding of the simplicity of the system.

I was in the property industry at the time and B.H bought a little cottage through me in February 2007. On the day of legal transfer, I met him at the property with a little gift (a pot plant) which was part of my usual customer care. Shortly afterwards, I made a "qualification call" as this was prior to my starting to use online surveys for this purpose. As he was highly likely to recommend me and my services, I also did the Client Multiplier Conversation at the same time. Note: This was an early version of the Referral Harvester. The Referral Harvester has been refined since, as described in this book. I no longer use telephone calls for qualification and only have the Client Multiplier Conversation at the next stage. But, at this time, it was all done at the same time.

My first Referral Harvester Action for this Advocate was on 15 February 2007. I sent a Personal Note and, as you can see in the image, I made a note to remind myself which card I sent him. You don't want to send the same card to an Advocate more than once!

About a month later, I found an article in a magazine, about preventing knee problems. The article was aimed specifically at marathon runners, which B.H. was. I sent him the article as a Valuable Item, knowing he would find it interesting. Running marathons was his main pastime and I knew this from the Client Multiplier Conversation we'd had before.

A few days later, B.H. gave me a referral. I thanked him and subsequently sold a lovely little house to his cousin. Note: Sometimes an Advocate will start referring to you immediately, as in this case, but sometimes it takes more time. Each Advocate is different and each business is different.

As you can see in the image, on 13 April I called my Advocate for a chat and made notes in my document to remind myself of all the main discussion points. These notes helped me a month later, when I sent him another Personal Note wishing him luck with an upcoming marathon. I knew he was going to be taking part in this particular marathon and thus had a great "topic" for a card. Later that month, B.H. gave me another referral which I thanked him for, followed up and again sold a property to his referral.

In June of that year, B.H. and I met at a local coffee shop for a Meet-Up. Again, I made notes in my document to remind myself of all the main topics of discussion. My next Referral Harvester Action was a phone call in mid-July. I asked him about his promotion and talked a bit about his new role and responsibilities.

B.H. remained one of my best Advocates until I left South Africa in 2008. You can see from my Referral Harvester Actions that it's all about building relationships. Focus on being interested in your Advocate. Build a relationship and the referrals will come.

The process – from beginning onward

After you have caught up with the "back-log" of current clients and your *Referral Harvester* is rocking and rolling, you need to work the system continuously. So let's summarise the entire process again for clarification.

A new client completes a transaction with you and your business. They are very happy because you have just solved a problem for them (provided that product or service they desperately needed). He / she immediately gets added to your Funnel spreadsheet. Within five days, you need to request that they complete a survey, either by sending them a link to an online survey or by phone (see Chapter 3). You will be checking survey results on a regular basis; I suggest at least once a week, depending on the volume of new clients you get every week. Within three days of receiving his / her survey results, the Funnel spreadsheet gets updated and the client is re-coded (see Chapter 2 for coding of clients).

If the survey results were less than desirable, your client care team needs to take action. If you received a positive result with an indication that the client would be willing to refer their contacts to you, you will need to take the next action. This is the step where you have the Client Multiplier Conversation with the client. This should ideally take place within five days of receiving the survey results. We don't want this new client to start forgetting about you! At this point you will also transfer this client to your CRM system (or whatever you use for your *Referral Harvester*).

Then the full force of your *Referral Harvester* kicks in. Within five days of having the Client Multiplier Conversation, you need to take your first *Referral Harvester* action. This could be any of the "touch" types we've discussed in Chapters 6 through 8. Personally, I prefer to send a hand written card as my first "touch". In it, I thank them again for their business and their willingness to refer their contacts to me. It is a nice, personal way to start building a new relationship. But, of course, it is entirely up to you which type of "touch" you want to start with.

Remember to update the client's details in your CRM system after each contact. Make short notes about what you did or any comments your client made. Use the reminder function in your CRM system to remind you to take the next *Referral Harvester* action in about 30 days' time. From there on, your Referral Harvester runs on autopilot. Every month, you will get a reminder to "touch" your client. In the figure below, you can see the entire process. You can also download this table from our website (www.talkingbusiness.biz/RH) to use as a sort of crib sheet while you are still getting used to the process.

Step	Timing	Action
1		Complete transaction
2	Within 5 days of Step 1	Send e-mail with link to survey
3	Within 3 days of getting results of Step 2	Update Filter Funnel – re-code client
4	Within 5 days of Step 3	Client Multiplier Conversation + update Filter Funnel
5	Within 5 days of Step 4	1st Referral Harvester Action (PN Recommended)
6	+- 30 Days after Step 5	2nd Referral Harvester Action
7	+- 30 Days after Step 6	3rd Referral Harvester Action
8	+- 30 Days after Step 7	4th Referral Harvester Action
9	+- 30 Days after Step 8	5th Referral Harvester Action
10	+- 30 Days after Step 9	6th Referral Harvester Action
11	+- 30 Days after Step 10	7th Referral Harvester Action
12	+- 30 Days after Step 11	8th Referral Harvester Action
13	+- 30 Days after Step 12	9th Referral Harvester Action
14	+- 30 Days after Step 13	10th Referral Harvester Action
15	+- 30 Days after Step 14	11th Referral Harvester Action
16	+- 30 Days after Step 15	12th Referral Harvester Action
17	+- 30 Days after Step 16	Repeat process from Step 5

It is a good idea to review your entire *Referral Harvester* list from time to time; possibly once a year. You might need to re-educate some clients or drop them from your elite club altogether. You will find a small proportion of would-be Advocates promise to refer their contacts to you, but never do. No amount of education will make a difference. This is a fact we need to accept and move on. Remember, people differ and you will not see the same results with every Advocate or would-be Advocate.

Chapter 10

Harvesting Time

When it comes to harvesting referrals from clients and contacts, the key is to be referable. This is an often overlooked point. You have to remember that people put their own credibility on the line each time they do a referral. If your client refers their mother-in-law to you and you give the mother-in-law bad service, what do you think the outcome will be? For your client, the mother-in-law and you? Firstly, your client will probably lose a great deal of credibility with his / her mother-in-law and never hear the end of it. I can guarantee you this client will not be inclined to refer anyone else to you either! Secondly, the mother-in-law will be less than impressed and quite possibly spread negative word of mouth about you and your business – and never do business with you again. Lastly, there is you. You have now not only lost the mother-in-law as a potential ongoing client, but probably also lost your original client. You will not receive any further referrals from this family and there might be negative word of mouth out there about you. The ripple effect of one negative interaction can be gigantic.

If you are going to make it your mission to harvest referrals, you need to be referable. You need to be absolutely certain that your level of service is as high as it can be. In fact, your service level should be such that your clients and their contacts are wowed by it. Go above and beyond. Be extraordinary. But this is basic business 101, isn't it?

The beauty of your *Referral Harvester* is that it has a built-in service checking system. By doing a survey of each new client (see Chapter 3) you will be getting constant feedback about your business, service and products. Use that feedback to constantly increase your service level. The survey gives you the opportunity to immediately spot a potential problem which allows you to rectify it before it grows into a massive issue. Don't waste these opportunities; leverage them to grow your business.

Don't let 'em marinade

Marinating is great – for certain foods – not people. When you receive a referral, you need to take action as soon as possible. Don't let it sit on your desk for days or weeks before contacting this new potential client. There might be some urgency and they need your product or service in quick time. If you don't take action, they might not bother to wait and find what they need elsewhere. And when they see your client again (the one who did the referral), they'll say: "No, your guy never bothered to contact me so I bought the widget elsewhere." Again, this reflects badly on you *and* your client. Chances are you might not receive another referral from him / her. Follow up on each referral as soon as you possibly can. It is part of being referable.

Show gratitude

We are leveraging an age-old, hard-wired culture in your *Referral Harvester*; that of obligation. It only makes sense then, to continue in the same vain and show gratitude.

Saying "thank you" when someone helps you or does you a favour, is the right thing to do. It is expected.

When you receive a referral from a client or contact, make sure you thank them – immediately. Don't wait until you bump into them again or until he / she asks you about it. Upon receipt, thank. Make it a rule in your business. It is a core part of making your *Referral Harvester* work. How you say "thank you" is entirely up to you. You could make a quick call, send an e-mail, thank them in person or send a personal note. It's doesn't matter, just show gratitude. This should not be counted as one of your 12 annual touches.

Your new business culture

You now have a well-oiled *Referral Harvester* working for your business 24/7. Each client who has gone through your education process will know about how you work and understand the key role referrals play in your business. It only makes sense then, to tell the rest of the world too!

You could add a tag line to your e-mail signature saying something like "I do business by referral. If you know of anyone who could benefit from my services, please put them in touch". Anyone receiving an e-mail from you will spot it and take note. I also know of people who have printed similar words onto their business cards. Another idea is to have stickers made, with a similar message, to stick onto the back of envelopes going out in the mail. Be creative, be different and get the message out there.

Be creative

Talking about being creative; don't feel you need to stick with only the "touches" I have mentioned in this book. Obviously it is vital to create the sense of obligation through cards, notes, Valuable Items and gifts. But think about different ways to "touch" your clients. Be unique.

One method I have been using recently is video mail. There are several online platforms you could use to send video mail to a client or contact. A short 10-second video is much more personal than the usual text based e-mail. I have used this method to thank clients for referrals or to send birthday messages. This is a great no-cost "touch" which will have a tremendous impact on your clients.

Your *Referral Harvester* is exactly that; yours. Use it however you want and mould it to your business style. Its use is not limited to your clients either. The system can be used for business contacts, collaborators and others too. Many of my clients have used their *Referral Harvester* to build strong relationships with contacts in closely-related industries. You'll be amazed at how many quality referrals you can harvest from contacts in closely-related industries. Financial advisors can feed referrals to will writers and accountants. Solicitors can pass referrals to financial advisors. Plumbers and electricians are perfect referral partners. The list goes on. Think about your own business and potential closely-related businesses. Who can you build a relationship with that will provide them *and* you with constant referrals?

It is harvesting time. Go out and harvest those referrals.

ABOUT THE AUTHOR

Tiana is a founding director of Talking Business Limited, a business development coaching and consulting company based in the North East of England. She works with organisations and individuals who are driven and ambitious and who have a burning desire to become the best in their field.

She specialises in the creation and implementation of systematic and strategic, goal-driven development plans and is results orientated, driven and focused. These attributes are downloaded to her clients' psyche through her no-nonsense approach.

Through her speaking engagements, seminars, workshops and coaching Tiana has helped countless business owners and managers on their journey to business success.

"You are where you are in business – and in life – due to one of two things; your actions or your inactions" – Tiana Wilson-Buys

Printed in Great Britain
by Amazon